Meat Market

Meat Market
Female Flesh under Capitalism

Laurie Penny

Winchester, UK
Washington, USA

O-Books is an imprint of John Hunt Publishing Ltd., Laurel House, Station Approach,
Alresford, Hants, SO24 9JH, UK
office1@o-books.net
www.o-books.com

For distributor details and how to order please visit the 'Ordering' section on our website.

Text copyright: Laurie Penny 2010
First Published 2011

ISBN: 978-1-84694-521-2

A CIP catalogue record for this book is available from the British Library.

Design: David Kerby

Printed in the UK by CPI Antony Rowe
Printed in the USA by Offset Paperback Mfrs, Inc

We operate a distinctive and ethical publishing philosophy in all
areas of our business, from our global network of authors to
production and worldwide distribution.

For my sisters, and for Mike

Acknowledgements

If I were to acknowledge everyone whose love and attention helped me write this there would be no space left for the chapters. Particular thanks, however, must go to:

James Butler, Roz Kaveney, Adrian Bott, Lucy Bond, Kerry Norman, Mark Brown, Sasha Garwood, Jess McCabe, Tanya Gold, Warren Ellis, China Mieville and my fairy godmother, Cath Howdle, for their editing input and moral support.

Andy May, Alex Betteridge and El Morris, three of the most excellent human beings I know, for their passion and friendship during the darkest parts of our early twenties.Chris Naden, for his tireless guidance and his wisdom.

Nina Power, for her searing feminist intellect and for introducing me to Zer0 Books. Tariq, Mark and Emma at Zer0, for putting up with my changing the title twenty times.

Germaine Greer, for responding to my enthusiastic ten-year-old correspondence so graciously.

My parents, Jane and Ray, for their patience and love; my little sisters, for giving me a reason to fight; and last but not least, to Michael Penny, who showed me where the books were.

Contents

Introduction
Branded Bodies

Why are we so afraid of women's bodies? Some four decades after women in most Western countries gained complete legal and equality, our societies continue to cultivate a rigorous, stage-managed loathing for female flesh. Whatever our age, race, physiotype and social status, women's bodies are punished and policed. We are bombarded every day with countless thousands of messages informing us that we do not look young enough, slim enough, white enough and willing enough, messages that come to us subtly and not so subtly, through film, television, advertising, print media and casual acquaintance, messages from which there is no reprieve. Corralled into rituals of consumption and self-discipline that sustain a bloated global market in beauty, diet, fashion and grooming products, three quarters of women in countries where food is plentiful go hungry every day in an effort to take up as little space as possible. Even if we do attain something close to the perfect physical control demanded of us, we are aware that our bodies are not our own: we are at constant risk of sexual violence and murder; one in five women in Britain and America is a victim of rape, and the rest of us learn to live in fear of rape. We are required to appear confident and sexually available at all times, but shamed and ostracised if we express arrogance, ambition or any sort of erotic desire. Everywhere, in every part of women's lives, physical control, self-discipline and sterile sexual display are the watchwords of a new gender conformity that is branded into our very flesh.

Female flesh is a powerful resource. Even in societies where women now have equality on paper, it is still women who are obliged to produce, bear and raise children and perform the majority of domestic and caring tasks entirely for free, often on top of full-time paid work outside the home. In addition, over 80% of everything that is sold in developed countries is bought by women[1], providing a vital engine for the consumption required to sustain neoliberal modes of production. Modern economies rely for their very survival upon women's paid and unpaid labour, purchasing power and reproductive capacity. That women should have this much power cannot be borne; the threat of revolt is too great.

If consumer society is to continue to exist in the manner to which it has become accustomed, it is essential that this latent power be appropriated, tamed and made docile. The ways in which contemporary capitalism undermines women's bodies, from advertising to pornography to the structures of gendered labour and domestic conflict, are not private troubles with no bearing upon the wider world. They are necessary fetters in a superstructure of oppression that has become so fundamental to the experience of femininity that it is effectively invisible. This superstructure is vital to the very survival of the patriarchal capitalist machine. If all women on earth woke up tomorrow feeling truly positive and powerful in their own bodies, the economies of the globe would collapse overnight.

This short book is an attempt to chart some of the ways in which women's bodies are marginalised and controlled under late capitalism. In four chapters, covering sexuality, eating disorders, gender capital and domestic labour, *Meat Market* sets out some of the parameters for the trade in female flesh as sexual and social capital, and demonstrates how women are alienated from their sexual bodies and required to purchase the fundamentals of their own gender.

In her criminally neglected *The Dialectic of Sex*, Shulamith Firestone identified this process as a campaign to alienate women from the "means of reproduction". Expanding on the work of Marx and Engels, Firestone advocated "a materialist view of history based on sex itself." It is just such a materialist vision of gender and society that *Meat Market* attempts to offer. What could be more material, after all, than the body and the idea of the body?

Meat Market does not waste time apologising for feminism or explaining why feminism remains a vital strand of thinking almost a century after women began to enfranchise themselves in the battle for the vote. Other books, essays and activist groups have already begun this work in the past five years, charting the emergence of a new generation of feminist agitators across the Western world and beyond. In a spirit of respectful enquiry, *Meat Market* devotes space to examining some of the analytical stumbling blocks of contemporary feminist thought, including a certain poverty of materialist analysis that stifles action and closes down debate. In particular, the questions of sex work and of the status of transsexual women within the movement are raised in the hope that feminism will soon be able to move towards a greater understanding of political totality and of the practical bases of women's oppression.

Meat Market is not a complete survey, nor one that exists in a vacuum. This book is a part of the new feminist movement, and it is indebted to the writing of bell hooks, Shulamith Firestone, Andrea Dworkin, Gloria Steinem, Germaine Greer, Nina Power and Naomi Wolf. Nobody has written about the marginalisation of Western women's bodies more powerfully than Wolf, whose lyrical description of the "iron maiden" of body and beauty fascism imposed upon women across the world suffers only from a hesitancy to relate the tyranny of beauty and bodily control to wider issues of labour, power and work, and to question the material basis of the idea of western femininity.

It is not enough to locate women's physical oppression in the sexual body, as many feminist thinkers have done. Sexual suppression, repression and oppression still occur, but they are only some of the strategies by which women's bodies are culturally policed as sites of potential rebellion. By the late 20th century, the partial dislocation of reproduction and labour from sexual intercourse following the widespread acceptance of contraceptive methods in most parts of the West had meant that post-Fordist capitalist control of women's gendered labour needed to be extended beyond the sexual and into the substantive, the nutritive and the semiotic architecture of gender and physicality itself.

Late capitalism quite literally brands the bodies of women. It sears its seal painfully into our flesh, cauterising growth and sterilising dissent. Femininity itself has become a brand, a narrow and shrinking formula of commoditised identity which can be sold back to women who have become alienated from their own power as living, loving, labouring beings.

From the moment we become old enough to want to own ourselves, the corporate cast of womanhood is stamped into our subconscious, burnt into our brains, reminding us that we are cattle, that we are chattel, that we must strive for conformity, that we can never be free. Not everything begins with sex, but this book does.

1
An Anatomy of
Modern Frigidity

Sex sells. That's our justification for everything. The sex industry has become every industry
Ariel Levy

The sexual bodies of women are out of control. Look around: teenagers who should be drinking lashings of ginger beer and going on picnics are wearing thongs and listening to Lily Allen. Children delinquently rummage in each other's pornographic pencil cases. Even babies are now born with the Playboy Bunny image tattooed onto their eyeballs. Their fault, the little tarts, for daring to look at the future.

Following the publication of Ariel Levy's *Female Chauvinist Pigs* in 2006, Western society finally arrived at the conclusion that the type of sexuality sold to young women in the 21st century might well be neither positive nor empowering. 'Raunch culture', as the mileu of lads' mags, go-go dancing and Girls Gone Wild has come to be known, is unquestionably a strategy of control. Patriarchal capitalism really does encourage young women to engage in a culture of monetised, deodorised sexual transaction in the name of 'choice' and 'empowerment', eliding the economic basis for all sexual work, paid or otherwise.

Resisting raunch culture, however, is not a complete answer to the marginalisation of female bodies in contemporary society. Skin mags and sexy dancing are symptoms of the problem, but they are not themselves the problem, and the strain of contemporary feminism that focuses its efforts on writing angry letters to the editors of magazines such as Nuts and Playboy is as flimsy as a stripper's discarded thong. To understand the mechanisms of objectification and bodily marginalisation that perpetuate women's struggle, we must cultivate a more ambitious vision of sexual dialectics.

The other side of sexualisation

The single story told about the sexuality of women today has them involved in a sort of abject whorishness. Adult society now acknowledges that having to grow up in a hailstorm of media messages encouraging female erotic availability might make life a little confusing for young women struggling with sexual feelings and anxious not to earn the shameful label of slut – but the same dialectic condemns young women as wanton strumpets, serial-shagging, binge-drinking and vomiting our worthless GCSEs into storm drains with our knickers around our knees. Apparently unable to glance at a glossy magazine without becoming pregnant, anorexic, or both, today's young women are imagined as special objects of pity and contempt. This gleeful horror at female promiscuity is peddled by right and left-wing pundits alike, and has little to do with feminism.

"There has been a change in the sexual behaviour of young women, but it isn't as dramatic as the media make out," said Dr Petra Boynton, a sex educator and academic. "Most young people still don't lose their virginity until they are over sixteen. If you take the generation who are now in their forties and fifties, many of them were having an awful lot of sex as young people, much of it unprotected sex. As adults we're very quick to look at young people and say, 'oh gosh, aren't they awful', but a lot of conversations that seem to care for young people actually end up being very moralistic about their behaviour, and start becoming discussions about what they should and should not wear, say and do."

There is, of course, a class element to this understanding of sexual victimhood. Hand-wringing tabloid articles about teenage pregnancy are invariably accompanied by model-posed photos of furiously smoking young women pushing prams around sink estates and scowling; in respectable magazines and political rhetoric, this translates to backhanded references to 'girls from deprived areas'. 'Sexualisation' is all well and good when middle-class parents order in crates of champagne for their teenagers' 'sweet sixteen' parties, but utterly deplorable when hip-hop-listening working class kids attempt to Get Their Freak On. "The perception is that it's only certain young girls who get pregnant," explains Boynton. "It's the bad teenage girls who get dressed up in short skirts and hit the town. Class is often associated with the worst aspects of negative sexual stereotyping."

In 2010, a British tabloid photographer snapped a picture of 20-year-old teaching assistant Sarah Lyons cavorting in Cardiff centre with a pair of pants around her ankles, and she temporarily became the face of female reprobation across the world. Never mind that she wasn't exposing any naughty bits; never mind that dancing with a pair of knickers around your ankles is perfectly legal behaviour; never mind that the pants in question weren't the ones she'd been wearing, but a comedy pair of David Hasselhoff knickers a mate had picked up in a bar. Never mind that poor Ms Lyons was on a course of antibiotics and was, in fact, stone-cold sober at the time: the new postergirl of binge-drinking man-women everywhere was suspended from her job pending a disciplinary inquiry, for the dubious crime of having fun in public.

The newspaper in question was NewsCorp's The Sun, whose famous page three section features topless glamour models every single day, part of a public dialectic which only has a problem with women dancing in their pants in public when they aren't getting paid to perform. In the storm of public moral approbation that followed, columnist Quentin Letts blamed feminism for spawning "an entire generation of loose-knickered lady louts".

"British girls have become fat-faced 'ladettes', goose pimples rising on the skin of their exposed thighs as they clack-clack-clack along the pavement en route to the weekend disco, destination bonk...Older generations would call these women 'slappers' – and they would be right."[2]

Not satisfied with fat-shaming, mocking women's bodies and clothes and branding us slags for any attempt to own our own sexual desire, Letts goes on to declare feminism the source of all social ills, taking detour after spluttering, purple-faced detour through teenage pregnancy, the decline of traditional marriage, drugs, free love and immigration as symptoms of this supposed pandemic of female degeneracy. It doesn't matter that the hordes of drooling young amazons apparently roaming the streets of our glorious nation in a savage rut of bleary, boozy, bottle-brandishing dick-frenzy aren't, actually, bothering anyone much: women still commit only 14% of violent crime in Britain and America, but we're still blamed for engendering social breakdown, when all we ever wanted to break down were creaking edifices of moral judgement and sexual repression.

The new fun police

This reanimated puritanism is thrown into ghoulish relief by an insistence on the absolute libertinism of modern culture, whereby any overt challenge to the erotic orthodoxy of the advertising and porn industries is seen as somehow 'anti-fun': a wearisome distraction from the emerging utopia of Western liberated hedonia. The frigidity of mercantile eroticism is the ghost at this feast, which is why nearly every public conversation about sexual morality fails to distinguish between consumer culture's brutally identikit traffic in sexual signs and sex itself. The assumption behind the sententious moral message preached by 'family values' spokespeople is that because we are surrounded by images of erotic capital, more actual sex, in the moist and panting sense, must be being had. This is in no way the case. What surrounds us is not sex itself but the illusion of sex, an airbrushed vision of enforced fun-fisting sexuality that is as sterile as it is relentless.

Advertising surrounds us with what are supposed to be images of sensual pleasure: from adverts for Herbal Essences to the iconic, forty-year campaign for Cadbury's Flake bar, white women's faces are caught in what we have come to understand as a rictus of simulated bliss, their eyes elegantly closed, perpetually turning away as if in embarrassment at the orgasmic effects of product X. But something is wrong with the picture. One of the finest modern acts of counter-culture in its purest sense is the website Beautiful Agony, a group project wherein anonymous contributors submit short videos of their faces at the point of orgasm. Watching hairy Australian biker dudes and grungy middle-aged ladies snarling, chuffing and grimacing like chimps in heat, one realises the magnitude of the lie being perpetrated by mercantile eroticism. The collected videos, hundreds of which are submitted every month, have one thing in common: none of them would make you remotely more likely to buy a bar of cornershop chocolate.

In Jean Baudrillard's assessment, the first task of sexual counter-culture under late capitalism must be

> to distinguish the erotic as a generalised dimension of exchange in our societies from sexuality properly so called. In the 'eroticised' body, it is the social function of exchange which predominates. The erotic is never in desire but in signs. This is where all modern censors are misled (or are content to be misled) – the fact is that in advertising and fashion naked bodies refuse the status of flesh, of sex, of finality of desire, instrumentalising rather the fragmented parts of body in a gigantic process of sublimation, of denying the body its very evocation.[3]

The 'fragmented parts of the body' that Baudrillard describes are a key feature of advertorial eroticism: disembodied parts, particularly of women, are fetishised as symbols of a sexuality that they cannot access. Shampoo suds run down naked torsos in soft-focus; lingerie is stretched over moronically thrusting groins; and everywhere, on book-covers and cereal packets and boxes of sanitary towels, disembodied legs in stilettoed high heels emblematise a cutesy, feminine consumer imperative that edges to replace genuine erotic impulse in as sincere a manner as that in which O'Brien in George Orwell's 1984 vowed that the party would destroy the orgasm. To paraphrase Orwell, if you want a vision of the future of feminism, imagine a high heel coming down on a woman's face - forever.

Learning erotic capital

The distinction that Baudrillard draws between erotic capital and sexuality itself must be understood as a real feature of contemporary sexual mores. Young people growing up with pressure to perform in every aspect of their lives find themselves aping a robotic capitalist eroticism that has little to do with their own legitimate desires.

I have a vivid memory of being impelled, as a grumpy fourteen-year-old, to take part in a musical competition with other girls in my school year in which we all performed a version of a popular music video in front of the rest of the school, in the name of 'House Spirit'. My vote was for the Offspring's "No Feelings", but it was eventually decided that we would all dress up in 'schoolgirl' outfits (as distinct from our actual uniforms) and attempt to recreate Britney Spears' "Baby, One More Time".

Those at a delicate stage of adolescence were provided with toilet-roll pneumatic breasts; we drew fake freckles on top of our real ones with biro and, when the day came, lip-synched along to the lyrics imploring a vague male cipher to perform unspecified acts of casual sexual violence. The crowd went wild. We hadn't been good; we hadn't even ballsed it up so concertedly badly that we deserved points for sheer shambolic brilliance. It was a whining, mal-coordinated pageant of teenage sexual mimicry made worse by the presence of three perky stage-school girls blowing bubblegum at the front row and flashing their knickers. Like Britney, who at the time had yet to commit the transgression of finishing puberty, we were a bizarre drag act riffing on a plasticized version of adult sexuality. We got the biggest cheer of the evening.

We were disqualified.

What our act expressed too vividly for the parent-judges to countenance was our innocent anxiety to involve ourselves in culture of mandatory sexual performance. We had learnt from an early age that our bodily desires were the lesser part of our sexual development: far more important, for young people, is the creation and maintenance of erotic capital.

Adolescent sexuality, as understood and marketed by older generations, has become a ritualised act of erotic drag: a grim, unsmiling duty of knowing looks, coquettish pouting and occasional listless fucking to be undertaken by any young person wishing to advance themselves socially – or economically. Young people are not merely in the thrall of a culture of porn and advertising that seeks to sexualise us; we have always been more than simply a target market. What many of us understand quite profoundly is that sexual performance and self-objectification are forms of work: duties that must be undertaken and perfected if we are to advance ourselves.

Pornography is a part of this language of erotic duty, and any discussion of the 'pornification' of contemporary youth culture must be understood in this context. The porn industry is worth some $14bn in America alone, and the explosion of online pornographic material freely available to young consumers provides a chorus for the consumer masquerade of paranoid, ritualised, repetitive heterosexuality. Feminist academic Dr Nina Power explains that "the early origins of cinematographic pornography tell a very different story about the representation of sex… one that is filled less with pneumatic shaven bodies pummelling each other into submission than with sweetness, silliness and bodies that don't always function and purr like a well-oiled machine."[4]

Power is right: when faces can be seen at all, nobody in modern pornography looks like they're having much fun.

The ubiquity of this blandly violent interpretation of pornography can be extremely bewildering for young people. Steeped in the shaming propaganda of our elders and bereft, for the most part, of any alternative educational or cultural models of sexuality, many of us begin our carnal adventures by attempting to reproduce the motifs of porn.

Young men as well as young women are undermined by this grinding, relentless erotic model. I know at least one young man who, during his first sexual experience with a woman, was horrified to discover that he had not been expected to pull out and ejaculate on his partner's face. He had understood from watching pornography that the experience was what all women wanted.

The formal rules of late capitalist pornography are the fulcrum of modern sexual affectlessness: an endless parade of disembodied cocks going into holes, a joyless, piston-pumping assembly line of industrial sexuality that seeks constantly to monetise new limits of 'hardcore', to milk more cum, to stretch sphincters wider and open orifices to double, triple, quadruple loads of faceless genital meat. Naomi Wolf described in 1991 how pornographic signs had come to "people the sexual interior of men and women with violence, placing an elegantly abused iron maiden into the heart of everyone's darkness, and blasting the fertile ground of children's imaginations with visions so caustic as to render them sterile. For the time being, the myth is winning its campaign against our sexual individuality."[5]

Entropy and irony

Much of the process by which the motifs of modern pornography have entered mainstream culture is excused by blithe claims on the part of producers and advertisers that this brutal objectification of young bodies is somehow 'ironic'. The excuse is feeble; the irony, however, is real. The pastiche of sexuality adopted by ambitious young people is nothing if not ironic: how could we be at all self-aware and not comprehend the blackly comic alienation of erotic work?

Irony is, in fact, one of the few authentic motifs of Western erotic culture in the early 21st century. A sort of kitsch, tongue-in-cheek naughtiness is relentlessly marketed at children and adults alike, from the peddling of 'Lolita'-themed bedspreads and schoolbags to the revival of 'burlesque' which has been translated from its roots in working-class protest theatre to a tastefully bourgeois package of sexual objectification, wrapped in feather-fans and expensive corsetry.

As popstars and presenters clamour for their turn with the nipple tassels, businesswoman and burlesque superstar Dita Von Teese extemporises on what she calls 'The Art of the Tease': "I sell, in a word, magic. Burlesque is a world of illusion and dreams and of course, the striptease.... As a burlesque performer, I entice my audience, bringing their minds closer and closer to sex and then -- as a good temptress must -- snatching it away."

The 'tease' is a cry from the heart of the capitalist sexual manifesto. What is sold is precisely illusion: a campy, peek-a-boo frigidity that leaves the consumer dazzled and insatiate.

Apologists for burlesque as an art form tend to enthuse about the 'empowering' nature of the 'tease', which lost all of its underground credentials the moment bourgeois gyms started offering keep-fit burlesque classes. Polestars, one of the largest companies to run such classes in the UK, claims to offer "a chance for the modern-day woman to learn the old art of seduction and improve your body... release your inner minx in saucy burlesque style!".

Sometimes one's inner minx just doesn't want to come out and play nicely. I lasted six months as a teenage burlesque dancer before all the saucy smiling started to make my face hurt.

Bunny and the brand

The sudden ubiquity of the Playboy Bunny logo perfectly exemplifies this cutesy alienation of marketable erotic signs from the sweaty reality of sex. In the early 21st century, the Bunny began an inexorable hop into the mainstream, appearing on pencil cases, hairslides and other products marketed at children. Feminist campaigners were the first to respond, with worthy projects such as "Bin the Bunny" attempting to educate young girls about the harmful nature of the porn industry; next, the family values brigade hijacked the Bunny as a symbol of moral decline. British Conservative leader David Cameron spoke out against the rabbit in his election campaign of 2010, explaining that "when you see a little girl wearing a T-shirt with a Playboy bunny, that's wrong, isn't it?"

But the Playboy empire itself has long been in decline. In the half-century since Gloria Steinem went undercover as a House Bunny to expose the mawkishly misogynist vision of white, submissive heteronormativity peddled by the playboy empire, Hefner has been far less successful as a pimp and pornographer than as a branding expert; even the revolving population of Playmates themselves are largely ignored by the popular press, the cotton-tail and flouncy ears looking droopy and dated in the harsh light of 21st-century celebrity. When, in 2009, the Playboy empire went up for sale, buyers were more interested in the logo than in the rest of the crumbling, impotent company: "there is more to this brand than just sex," Kelly O'Keefe, a branding specialist at Virginia Commonwealth University, told Reuters. "There is sophistication, there is lifestyle, and there is freedom."

Sophistication, lifestyle and freedom are worlds away from the fumbling, awkward, sticky revelations that necessarily accompany one's first decade of sexual experience. Fantasy is, of course, deeply implicated in the physicality of sex, which takes place at the panting border between dream and secretion, but the Playboy Bunny emblematises the absolute dislocation of fantasy from physical fact.

The Bunny brand is a Lacanian play of signs bouncing blithely away from any signifiable sexuality.

It can hardly be argued that the ubiquity of the Playboy Bunny logo or its popularity with young girls are positive developments, but it must be understood that what is being objected to here, as elsewhere, is not sex, but symbol: the black-and-white, lipless, featureless symbol of a perky, prosthetic sexuality whose alienation from the flesh and intimacy of real sex can be mass-produced. At root, Bunny orthodoxy is repulsed by human personality, as Hefner himself explained: "Consider the kind of girl that we made popular: the Playmate of the Month. She is joyful, joking, never sophisticated... we are not interested in the mysterious, difficult woman."

The Bunny symbolises erotic capital as distinct from the lived experience of flesh. As a sign, it overwhelms the sexual encounters it has come to signify. A 2010 survey of unmarried Americans between 18 and 29 revealed that many have little knowledge of even common contraceptive methods such as condoms and the pill, but when we first saw the Bunny on our lunchboxes, we had a naughtily amorphous understanding of what it was supposed to mean. And one thing is certain: when a fifty-year-old rubber-stamp rabbit in a bow-tie becomes an internationally recognised sign for the mummy-and-daddy dance, it's safe to say that something has gone horribly wrong with our understanding of sexuality.

Starving hearts

What is at play here is a horror of flesh: a rubberised capitalist repugnance for the meat and intimacy of human sexuality. Modern censors are necessarily misled about the nature of consumer frigidity, because their complicity is a necessary part of the trick: the strategic alienation of sexual consumers from their erotic selves relies precisely on censorship to blur the distinction between sexual intimacy and erotic capital, only one of which can be mass-produced. Such a joyless vision of eroticism only looks edgy and exciting because the young and randy have nothing else to work with.

Antiquated paradigms of sexual morality policed the sexuality of young people with a variety of instruments of rusty erotic torture, from tight-laced steel corsets to spiked genital casings designed to prevent young men from masturbating. Our liberated, libertine age of funtime mercantile eroticism requires us to internalise the corset and the spikes; to starve, suffer, spend, primp and perform, to take our place in a monetised pageant of sexual scarcity when, in fact, we have always lived in an age of erotic abundance.

The ooze and tickle of realtime sex, which can neither be controlled nor mass-produced and sold back to us, threatens both capital and censorship. Shaming the choices of young people whilst bombarding us with pounding, plasticised, pornified visions of alienated sexuality creates an impression of sexual scarcity that serves both agendas. But if human beings own anything by right and birth, we own an abundance of flesh, an abundance of dirt and sex and sublimity. Only by embracing this abundance can we liberate ourselves.

The eroto-capitalist horror of human flesh, and of female flesh in particular, is a pathology that can and must be resisted. If we are to free ourselves from this pernicious fear of flesh, we have to learn to live in our own meat. We have to reject the narrow coffin of performance and perfection laid out for young women and increasing numbers of young men, and learn to evoke and respond to our own desires. If we are ever to achieve real sexual freedom, we must be brave enough to resist the ruthless logic of performative erotic irony.

A new model of corporate puritanism is on the march, and what is being censored on all sides is precisely Baudrillard's "evocation of the body". The Western female body, which seems to be everywhere on display, is in fact marginalised and appropriated by a culture of monetised sexuality that alienates us from our authentic personal and political selves.

A note on whores and whorishness

If we are to properly understand women's oppression in the West today, objectification and sexual performance must be understood as work. The sexual sell is real labour, propping up a socially mandated measure of erotic capital. From the working hours devoted to the purchase and strategic application of clothes and hair and beauty products, to the actual labour of dieting and exercise, to the creation and maintenance of sexual persona, self-objectification is work, first and foremost. Female sexuality, which every day becomes increasingly synonymous with objectification, is work. And it is impossible to talk about sexuality as work without talking about sex work itself.

One of the supreme ironies of Western gender production is that whilst the sexual sell is everywhere, the sale of sex itself still takes place in a shadowy underworld of social taboo, criminal activity and violence. One can market one's sexuality and labour to increase erotic capital in the workplace, but prostitutes – the overwhelming majority of whom are women servicing men – are still amongst the most vulnerable and marginalised members of society. Women who do not or cannot compete in the cultural meat market and sell themselves as sexy face social consequences – but the worst thing one can call a woman is 'whore.'

The contemporary feminist conversation about sex work is a sea of unheard voices, private tragedy and misinformation in which moral squabbling obscures the real-life concerns of many vulnerable women. The net result of continued ideological wrangling between feminists, sex workers' rights activists and misogynist lawmakers has left the legal status of sex work in Britain and America an unworkable, precarious Jenga tower of muddled laws and moral equivocation, wherein women who work as prostitutes are stranded in a socio-economic no man's land, their work just about legal enough to offer a seedy but acceptable outlet for restrained bourgeois sexual mores and an economic option for women in desperate financial circumstances, and just about illegal enough that the market for commercial sex remains illicit and underground, depriving sex workers of public dignity and of the full protection of the justice system, and satisfying the prudish public drive to punish those who sell sex.

The recent resurgence in the feminist movement in Britain in particular has seen issues such as abortion rights and the pay gap elbowed out in favour of monolithic tub-thumping about sex work. The argument has descended into a stark moral binary between a vision of sex work as an activity wholly based on free choice or – the more common feminist viewpoint – wholly exploitative. "Equality for women is a farce in a society where it is considered normal for men to buy our bodies," said Finn MacKay of the Feminist Coalition Against Prostitution. "We can't be free while so many of us are literally for sale. As long as I believe prostitution is a form of violence against women, then how can I work alongside anyone who promotes it as a job like any other?"

The clunky notion that prostitution is itself violence against women – even, presumably, when both parties are male – obstructs more useful analysis. Only when one acknowledges that sex can, in theory, be sold without exploitation can one ask why it so rarely is, even in the richest societies on earth.

Prostitution is still one of the most dangerous, stigmatised and poorly rewarded jobs that a person can do. Violence is done to sex workers by pimps, johns and punters as well as by the state in the form of police coercion. The marginalisation of the labouring bodies of sex workers is an extreme form of the marginalisation of the labouring bodies of all women. For that reason, the extension of workers' rights to all those who sell sex should be a point of urgency for feminist activists.

The first point of resistance must, of course, be greater legal protection for those who sell sex. Even the most ideologically divided of activists can agree on this point. In an article for the Guardian in 2010, Thierry Schaffauser, a sex worker and union activist, and

Cath Elliott, an abolitionist feminist, concluded that "whilst we've all been busy arguing over other things, those most in need of our help continue to suffer violence. We believe the criminalisation of sex workers/prostitutes helps to legitimise those who attack them. Criminalisation of soliciting is a sexist law."[6]

In recent years, a slew of books and television programmes such as Tracy Quan's *Diary of a Manhattan Call Girl* have made great show of bringing prostitution out of the shadows when, in fact, something quite different is going on. The prostitution celebrated by pop culture is bourgeois prostitution – 'high-class' prostitution, as the tabloids like to call it – eliding the experiences and needs of the majority of sex workers, most of whom are not bourgeois.

Dr Brooke Magnanti of Bristol was recently forced to out herself as *Belle de Jour*, the former PhD student and prostitute behind the blog which turned into the book which turned into the lucrative, trashily unchallenging ITV adaptation, *Secret Diary of a Call Girl*, in which Billie Piper wears a variety of rump-revealing latex dresses and does a lot of heavy breathing. The show, now in its third series, has become the dominant vehicle for the Belle De Jour meme, stripping out everything that was realistic and challenging about Dr Magnanti's blog and leaving a deodorised husk of middle-class male fantasy in which a massively undercast Piper perkily advises the audience to "work out what the client wants, and give it to him as quickly as possible".

The glamorisation of bourgeois prostitution, alongside complete popular indifference to making sex work any safer or more legal, betrays a persistent patriarchal anxiety to maintain a status quo that constrains and commodifies female sexuality. This easy structure of umbrage and oppression hardly offers an answer to people like Rebecca Mott, a former prostitute and abolitionist activist:

> "The torment of being prostituted has never left me. On the first night, when I was fourteen, I was gang-raped for many hours. That was the test to see if I was suitable material for prostitution. You learn that your body is there to be damaged.

That you have no right to say no. That your purpose is to service men in any and every way they can think of. It is so much easier to speak only of women who appear in charge of their own working environment, rather than the reality."

The main element missing from the contemporary conversation about prostitution, as ever, is class. The one thing that almost no-one has asked about Belle De Jour is why a PhD student might find herself selling sexual intercourse to fund her studies in the first place. Commentators are slow to connect the glamorous fantasy of Belle with a bankrupt higher education system in which indebted students routinely live well below the poverty line to afford the degrees their future employers increasingly demand. In 2010, a report by Kingston University suggested that since the abolition of the student grant, the number of British students funding their degrees by working as prostitutes and strippers had increased fivefold.[7]

Sex work is an economic question, not a moral one: in a world where shame and sexual violence are still hard currency, the normalisation of the sex industry is a symptom not of social degeneration, but of the economic exploitation of women on an unprecedented scale, in a feminised labour market where all working women are expected to commodify their sexuality to some extent. The violence done to the bodies of sex workers and the moral marginalisation of prostituted women impacts on all women, everywhere.

The ubiquity of female sex work as fact and as social narrative affects women who are not sex workers, because under late capitalism, *all female sexuality is work*. The labouring sexual bodies of prostitutes are hated, feared and punished by society at large as part of a culture that understands female sexual objectification as labour whilst remaining terrified of the notion of women gaining real control over the proceeds of that labour. Why else has the idea of 'pimping' become a shorthand for cool over the past decade? Women must remain alienated from the means of sexual labour and reproduction, so it is vital that we remain alienated from our sexuality, even if it's our main means of survival in the meat market of modern capitalism. Popular culture reminds women that the sale of sexual signs is precarious as well as crucial, and that even if we get it completely right – even if we work out how to give the clients exactly what they want – we will never be allowed to own our sexual bodies.

2
Taking Up Space

Female hunger – for public power, for independence, for sexual gratification – must be contained. On the body of the anorexic woman such rules are grimly etched
Susan Bordo

We live in a world which worships the unreal female body and despises real female power. In this culture, where women are commanded to always look available but never actually be so, where, where we are obliged to be appear socially and sexually consumable whilst consuming as little as possible, our most drastic retaliation is to undertake our own consumption: to consume ourselves – and so we do, in ever-increasing numbers.

One in every hundred women and girls and one in every thousand men in the West suffers from a serious eating disorder: a private, violent expression of the cultural trauma whereby the female body is appropriated as a market resource, where women themselves are fashioned as industrial inputs. Since 1999, there has been an 80% rise in the number of teenagers admitted to hospital with anorexia nervosa; across Europe and America, one in every hundred young women and one in every thousand young men has the disease. Roughly double those numbers suffer from bulimia nervosa or other pathologically disordered eating patterns. One in ten young sufferers will die from the direct effects of the disease, and over half will never recover, living with years of complications and, in many cases, choosing to take their own lives.[8] That women suffer from eating disorders in overwhelming numbers is evidence not of the fragility of the sex but of the toxicity of patriarchal capitalist standards of femininity after nearly a century of political feminism. Every day it is made clear to us that we are hungrier, messier, uglier, needier, angrier, more powerful and less perfect than we ought to be. It is far harder to challenge that culture of criticism and the low self-esteem it promotes than to simply starve away the shame. Eighty years after universal suffrage was granted in most of the developed world, in a generation which has seen women's power and stature and opportunities grow and grow, we have been persuaded in greater and greater numbers to slim down, to take up less space, to shrink ourselves.

The triumph of self-starvation represents a major defeat of feminism in the West. All aspects of the phenomenon are gendered – from the everyday campaigns of self-hatred embarked on by up to 75% of women daily in the name of dieting, to the thousands of women and men worldwide starving themselves to death in the midst of plenty. The unbearable, contradictory pressures of gender weigh particularly heavily upon women and on queer, homosexual and bisexual men and women, which may account for the fact that an estimated 25% of women and 50% of men who have eating disorders are not heterosexual.[9] The idea of eating disorders as a by-product of celebrity culture is belied by the cruel and radical complexity of the mindset. Jo, now 23, became anorexic at sixteen: "My mother thought I wanted to be thin so I could get a boyfriend. Ha! In fact, reason number one behind my drive to be thin was that I didn't want to look like a real girl; I didn't want to be looked at by men in the street; I hated my breasts and my soft round curvy girly parts because that just didn't feel like me. It still doesn't. The anorexia...that was me wanting to be as sexless as I could possibly manage to become."

Tradition has it that women do everything, including starve themselves to death, in an effort to look good and attract a man – but the idea that eating disorders are solely an effect of beauty culture is disingenuous and demeaning to sufferers. The pain is visceral, it is political, and it is as much a reaction against the insistent labour of beauty fascism as submission to objectification. Hannah, a ferociously bright 22-year-old studying Economics at Cambridge, did not starve herself because she wanted to be beautiful: "Anorexia has nothing to do with wanting to look pretty. In fact, I knew I looked worse at lower weights. I wanted to look disgusting and ugly. I wanted my heart to sputter and stop and my bones to thin, my organs to give up on me. If I had a heart attack caused by starvation, maybe that wouldn't really count as suicide."

There is something paradoxically feminist about the violent inverted logic of eating disorders – a desperate and deadly psychological stand-in for the kind of personal and political freedoms we have not yet achieved. Women and girls who have been denied their own autonomy find a measure of that autonomy in the physical and psychological self-destruction of eating disorders: a rebellion by self-immolation, by taking society's standards of thinness, beauty and self-denial to their logical extremes. Hundreds of thousands of women, as I write, are destroying themselves in pursuit of this pyrrhic victory – and Western society, fostering a deep loathing for female flesh, applauds them for doing so.

Saintly starving sisters

In 1991, Naomi Woolf described in *The Beauty Myth* how the epidemic of eating disorders plaguing the women of the west had been ignored by the media and governments, rightly identifying the omission as evidence of the sexist priorities of healthcare and strategists across the world. This is no longer the case.

Two decades on, the same culture is saturated with films, books, documentaries, plays and endless harrowing newspaper articles all claiming to 'expose' eating disorders – chiefly anorexia, the more glamorous and alien sister in the toxic family of deadly gendered disorders. Open any magazine, click on any gossip website, and you'll find speculations on the latest celebrity's suspected bulimia running alongside columns on what Madonna doesn't have for breakfast these days. The media has turned anorexia and bulimia into the diseases of the moment – gruesome and disgustingly cool, evidence of the supposed fragility and incompetence of successful women in the public eye.

Concern for the mental and physical health of the youth of tomorrow is clearly not the priority here. In fact, recent attempts by the international media to 'raise awareness of the dangers' of eating disorders have looked less like a genuine campaign than a series of mad, gory collisions between a famine relief documentary and a porn movie. In the promotional posters for the 2008 ITV documentary *Living With Size Zero*, a model with rake-thin limbs stands with one leg cocked on a set of scales, wearing nothing but skimpy underwear and pouting provocatively at the camera, aping a sexual attraction her emaciated body appears to bechemically unable to produce. A tape measure is wound tightly around her torso. This is not 'raising awareness' – this is idolatry.

The 'size zero' woman is a capitalist fantasy of subsumed femininity, a media fiction spawned in the twisted imaginations of fashion editors and tabloid shysters - and a dangerous fiction, at that. It's a fiction that perpetuates tired gender stereotypes and feeds back into the cannibalistic ethos of the fashion industry. It's a fiction that centres upon the degrading idea that women are stupid, frivolous and impressionable. And it's a fiction that undermines the seriousness of the real epidemic of eating disorders that is devastating the lives of women across the world.

The 'size zero debate'- referring to the American clothing size 0, the equivalent of a UK women's dress size four or an European 32, indicating a body-mass index typical of a severely underweight young woman- has been raging since August 2006, when two South American models, Luisel Ramos and Ana Carolina Reston, died from the effects of starvation-diets designed to keep their weight horrifically low. In response to the tragedies, Madrid Fashion Week 2006 banned models with a body-mass index lower than 18 from the catwalk, and since then many fashion houses, celebrities and designers have made statements opposing the use of unhealthily underweight models in the industry.

It's a story with all the classic ingredients of a good scoop: it has the glamour of high fashion, the tantalising whiff of institutional conspiracy, and, of course, the tragically premature deaths of gorgeous young women. Conveniently, it also cries out to be illustrated with ogle-worthy shots of stick-thin, half-naked teenagers.

The 'size zero' myth is largely irrelevant to the vast majority of sufferers from eating disorders who are not catwalk models or fashion heiresses. Meanwhile, the number of women and, more invisibly, of men with the disorders continues to grow. The charity Beat estimates that there are 165,000 people with serious eating disorders in the United Kingdom alone, and they are outnumbered many times over by the millions who, whilst not technically eating disordered, live their lives in a permanent state of shame, self-denial and yo-yo dieting; by the thousands of harassed middle-aged women who have gone hungry for decades as the imperative to hate their own beautifully aging bodies grows ever louder; by the thousands of teenage girls who would rather cut short their lives by years and risk painful death by suffocation than chance the weight gain associated with quitting smoking. Schooled by the circumspective propaganda of the fashion, diet, beauty, music, media and pornographic industries, women in the early 21st century have learned to despise their own flesh. The discrepancy between the dogged models of erotic and social self-fashioning offered to us and the reality of our everyday lives and developing bodies can be almost unbearable. Celebrities and fashion models who are tacitly understood to be engaged in a prolonged process of self-starvation, seem to promise to teach us both how to be desired and how to disengage from our bodily desires. It is easy to ache for the perfect control they seem to embody, to yearn to be the ubiquitous object rather than an abject consumer. It is easy to learn not to want anything: easy to play the rules to their ultimate, tragic conclusion and refuse to consume anything, to punish the body and murder the sex drive with the artificial pre-pubescence chemically created by starvation. Easier to become a sign rather than attempt to signify anything. Easier, ultimately, to die.

The chemistry of control

Enforcing thinness is an ideal way to control powerful women on the cusp of liberating themselves, because eating disorders are that rare thing: political and cultural disorders with deep physiological effects. It would be disingenuous to discuss the political ramifications of eating disorders on our gender ideologies without acknowledging the medical basis for these conclusions.

Anorexia nervosa is the most lethal of all mental illnesses precisely because its physical and psychological effects are so profoundly entangled. It has been conclusively proved that prolonged starvation can actually provoke many of the symptoms of anorexia nervosa, causing sufferers to obsess over food and become depressed, self-destructive and suicidal. In 1944, for instance, researchers at the University of Minnesota enlisted and systematically starved 36 conscientious objectors – all healthy adult men with no psychiatric problems. Over the course of a year, the men lost 25% of their body weight, and were then fed normally again – with staggering results. All of the participants quickly began to display unusual psychological symptoms. They became highly distressed, agitated and bewildered, and developed bizarre rituals around eating, collecting recipes and hoarding food obsessively – not just during the experiment but, in some cases, for the rest of their lives.[10]

One of the participants, Harold, told researchers in 2006 that the experiment was highly distressing "not only because of the physical discomfort, but because ... food became the one central and only thing really in one's life. I mean, if you went to a movie, you weren't particularly interested in the love scenes, but you noticed every time they ate and what they ate." The men became extremely disturbed by the idea of weight gain, and their reactions included pathological self-harm. One participant amputated three of his own fingers with an axe.

Unless you've been very hungry for a long time yourself, you can't imagine what prolonged malnutrition does to your mind – never mind how obsessive you started off, you'll soon start thinking in tiny repetitive circles about everything. You'll become anxious, tearful, constantly on edge, and this is an evolved reaction – in response to what it perceives as famine, the lizard-brain becomes hyper-focused, wanting you to stay awake searching for something, anything, to eat. Little habits, distractions – smoking, gum-chewing, booze, caffeine, uppers – become addictions. You can't sit still, you can't concentrate. You become angry, irrational, paranoid, fearful. Your grades and work performance start slipping, you've lost all your hopes and ambitions, because all you can think about is food and how to avoid it. You can feel your thoughts moving more slowly, like in those dreams when you're running through thick sludge away from some nameless terror. All the while, part of you feels invincible. You feel that you might perform any physical or intellectual feat, running a marathon or writing a symphony or hammering in railroad tracks – when in reality you have made yourself socially and functionally useless. You have taken the work of self-negation and under-consumption that promised to make you the perfect worker, the perfect student, the perfect wife, but in doing so you have destroyed your capacity to work or love or function in society in any sustained manner.

All of these are merely the physiological effects of prolonged starvation. But this is the state to which a culture saturated with dieting imperatives, rake-thin role models and liposuction adverts on bus hoardings attempts to reduce its most powerful women and an increasing number of its young men. The perverse and pervasive rhetoric of thinness is an enforced surrendering of personal power – the shame and discipline of the patriarchal capitalist conception of women forcibly enacted on the body in the cruellest and most insulting of ways.

Personal/political

Making rhetorical points which start with the phrase "when I was anorexic" is always fraught with difficulty. How can I talk about the real, messy human pain of disintegration and recovery without making myself sound attention-seeking? It's almost impossible, so I want to make one thing perfectly clear: I am not proud of my anorexia. When I look back at the years I wasted starving myself to the point of death, what I feel is anger, resentment and shame. It was a miserable time. No pictures of me remain from that time, and if they did you still wouldn't be getting to see them, because they would show you nothing new: by now we all know what anorexia looks like. I was not a special and fragile princess. I was a stupid, suicidal child, and I nearly broke my family's heart.

I say this not out of masochism, but because somebody needs to tell the truth. The trivialisation of women with eating disorders in the popular press – painting us at once as helpless victims and as silly little girls obsessed with celebrity – does a great disservice to women and to people of all genders who struggle to feed themselves. Women are not powerless beings without agency, even in this circumscribed culture, and only by acknowledging that fact will we ever achieve full adult emancipation, or ever save ourselves from the hell of narcissistic self-negation. We need to take responsibility for our part in the cruel machine of enforced feminine starvation psychosis. To do anything else would be to accept our own victimhood.

I can't remember the precise moment when I became addicted to avoiding food. At 16, I was unhappy at school, my parents were getting divorced, and I was sickened by the urgency of the desires I felt, not just for food but for love, sex, work, excitement — normal human needs that I had learned were dangerous and wicked.

I decided that it would be simpler to train myself not to want anything at all. At first, I cut out chocolate and treats; then it was carbohydrates and dairy, then breakfast, lunch and dinner.

As my adolescent puppy fat began to pour away, friends and

family complimented my new figure, reinforcing the message that good girls don't eat. I felt light, pure and virtuous. It felt good; I wanted more. I started to spend hours doing strenuous exercise to burn off extra calories after school, and kept the supermodels' motto "nothing tastes as good as skinny feels" scratched into my hand to remind me that giving in to the terrible hunger pangs I felt was a sign of weakness. By the time I was 17, I was in hospital, so malnourished that I weighed less than a four-year-old.

Because eating disorders are associated with fashion, it's easy to believe that anorexia is a glamorous illness, a lifestyle choice made by rich or famous women whose only concern is to be thin enough to fit into next season's tiny frocks. But there's nothing glamorous about spending every waking second so hungry that you can barely stand. At no point, in the depths of my illness, did I crouch over a service station toilet bowl with two fingers down my throat, forcing myself to vomit up slimy lumps of the cracker I'd eaten for dinner and think, hey — I'm living the dream.

The reality of life with anorexia is very far from a catwalk. The daily squelch and grind of an eating disorder is not only disgusting — it's also deeply boring. My little sister, who was 12 at the time, told me: "You were no fun at all when you were ill. You were always talking about food, and even when you didn't it was obvious you were thinking about it. It was just miserable to be in the same room as you, to be totally honest. You just weren't you."

When you are anorexic, your world shrinks to the size of a dinner plate. You withdraw from your friends and family, you forget about the music and books and politics you used to love, you can't concentrate on anything except where your next meal isn't coming from. You tell yourself that nothing tastes as good as skinny feels, but by the time you've made yourself that skinny, you've lost the ability to feel anything at all.

Hospital was terrifying: the unfamiliar ward, the endless medical tests, the locks on the doors. The girl in the room next door, Lianne, was once a promising chemist; she used to spend her days cutting out pictures of fashion models for her scrapbook with an intravenous drip hooked to her wrist.

At the end of my first week in hospital, Lianne ripped the feeding tube out of her wrist and ran away from the ward, determined to end her life. She was so weak that she collapsed on the bus into town. As I watched the ambulance pull up underneath my window, returning Lianne to hospital, I realised that I had a choice: I could either choose to stay ill and become like Lianne, living out a withered, damaged half-life of hospital stays and self-starvation, or I could dare to contemplate the possibility of a different life. That night, I ate my first proper meal in more than two years.

Starting to eat again is extremely difficult when a part of you believes that you deserve to starve. It's even more difficult when you're surrounded by images of women who look just as scrawny and miserable as you do and told that this is the ideal to which you should aspire. The softer and curvier my body became, the more outsized I felt; compared to the perfect models on the cover of every magazine, the meat and stink of my new body disgusted me. But somehow, out of sheer bloody-mindedness, I clung on. No matter how repulsed I felt, I kept on eating my meals with the joyless efficiency of a robot. I had decided to try to find something that tasted better than skinny felt.

Recovery from an eating disorder is difficult to measure, because it involves so much more than putting on weight: you have to will yourself to believe that you deserve your place in the world, the whole mess and hunger of your flesh and brain and lust and ambition. Even when you hate your normal-sized body so much that you want to tear chunks out of it, you have to get up, eat your meals and get on with your day. You have to learn to say those two, terrifying little words: I'm hungry.

These days, I'm always hungry — sometimes for a sandwich, sometimes for sex, or work, or travel, or a change; sometimes I just want someone to hug. I've learned that it's OK not to be a good little girl, that it's OK to break the rules, even when you are told that you ought to take up as little space as possible. I refuse to shrink myself to fit into the narrow coffin that society lays out for young women. From time to time, I still miss my eating disorder. I miss the sense of control that comes when avoiding food is your highest ambition. But today, after three years of recovery, I have a degree, a career and a huge appetite for adventure. I'm hungry, too hungry to go back, to ravenous and insatiate to submit and pare myself down again. I'm hungry, still hungry, and the flesh and disappointment of real life taste better than skinny ever felt.

Fear and loathing

Fear of female flesh and fat is fear of female power, the sublimated power of women over birth and death and dirt and sex. In his essay *The Roots of Masculinity*, therapist Tom Ryan notes that "Most therapists have frequently heard complaints from men about fears of being dominated, controlled, swallowed up or suffocated. Underlying these fears…is a more basic fear about the disintegration of maleness. … Dave, a thirty year old professional man, wishes his partners to be 'firm and sharp'. There must be no hint of softness or largeness, particularly in the breasts. On occasions when Dave has seen or been with a 'fat' or 'large' woman, he experiences a sensation of being lost or enveloped by their 'layers of flesh'."[11]

Over the course of the 20th century, escalating female emancipation has offset by a growing taboo against female corpulence – not just of women who are overweight, but of any female fat, anywhere. Cellulite, saggy bellies, fat around the arms, natural processes which affect all female bodies, even the leanest, after puberty, are particularly loathed. Where female bodies are permitted, they must be as small and as 'sharp' as possible. The threat that patriarchal birthright will be 'swallowed up or suffocated' by gender equality is made manifest in the fear of female fat, and that phobic response to the reality of physical femaleness has been internalized by women and men across the western world. As soon as the female child becomes aware of her physical and spiritual self, she learns that her self is excessive, and must be contained.

It is not coincidental that contemporary media fascination with eating disordered female celebrities is explicitly set against the success of women in the public eye. It is not enough for women such as Victoria Beckham and Angelina Jolie to be preternaturally thin; they must be seen to be suffering to be thin, to be starving themselves, so that their starvation and suffering overwhelms their personal success in the popular imagination of their personae. Conversely, the actress Keira Knightley, whose slender frame is by all accounts a fluke of genetics, has been forced to spend a great deal of her career refuting claims that she is anorexic. In 2007 Knightley successfully sued the Daily Mail newspaper for suggesting that she had anorexia or a similar eating disorder, and had lied to the public about it.

Riot, don't diet

Society needs to acknowledge women's hunger. Not just our hunger for the 2,500 calories a day we need to fuel us through full and interesting lives, but our hunger for life, for love, for expansion of our horizons, our hunger for passionate politics, our hunger to take up space and to live and act out of our own flesh. Public horror of female meat, society's sick fascination with eating disorders, is part of a structure of patriarchal capitalist control grounded on horror of women's physical power.

Feminine advice-manuals from Cosmopolitan to the 12th-century nuns' handbook Ancrene Wisse have encouraged self-denial as a watchword and guiding principle, apart from in certain explicit avenues such as, variously, the January sales or the love of Jesus. Women are still expected quite literally to deny themselves: to erase their personhood and throw over the wants of the body and the hunger of the soul for transformation. The adventure of being fully human, however, cannot be achieved simultaneously with the denial of the self – and it is this denial of female selfhood, this denial of the dirt and ooze of female power, that feminists of all genders and stripes must resist if we are to root out the deepest lines of misogynist resistance in our societies.

Society cannot grow and develop if it continues to insist that one half of its citizens spend their energies physically and psychologically shrinking themselves. But reclaiming the flesh is about radical surrender to female power, and this will be as hard for many women, grown used to denying and paring down their bodies and their selves, as it will be for the men who must make room for those bodies and those selves. This strategy goes far beyond individual women leaning to love their bodies. Empowerment is about far more than physical self-confidence, whatever the cosmetic surgery industry may claim.

Perhaps the cruellest of all tricks played on women by contemporary consumerism is the tendency over the past five years for popular culture to appropriate women's anxiety over taking up social space in order to sell them circumscribed solutions. Even as dieting is sold as the ultimate way for women to positively transform their lives, TV programmes like Britain's *How to Look Good Naked* prey on those same fear by suggesting that all women really need to feel free from the tyrannies of body fascism is a really great bra and the chance to stand on a stage and be judged approvingly by men.

When I began to eat again and started to approach a healthy weight, I was bombarded with compliments. The few friends I hadn't managed to alienate through years of self-starvation rushed to reassure me that I was more attractive as a size eight than I had been as a size zero. I went to bed with men who told me that they loved my curves, thinking that this was what I wanted to hear. I tried desperately hard to love my curves, too – but the real breakthrough came when I stopped defining myself merely by my dress size. Once

I started to believe that my worth as a person had nothing to do with how my body looked to other people, I began to give myself permission to take up the space I needed and claim the power I craved.

Fear of female flesh is fear of female power, and reclaiming women's bodies must go hand in hand with reclaiming women's power. This cannot be achieved simply by purchasing expensive body lotion. Men and women alike need to confront our fear of female flesh, to risk being overwhelmed by the power of women to change society and take charge of their own lives. All we need to do is acknowledge how hungry we are for that future to arrive, and take the first bite.

3
Gender Capital

Sex class is so deep as to be invisible.
Shulamith Firestone

The eroto-capitalist fear of female flesh has translated into a fight for gender itself. What is girlhood, after all, but shoes, clothes and conspicuous consumption? When femininity is intimately tied into the labour of objectification, the cues of gender itself can be bought and sold on the labour market. As such, any woman wishing to free herself from the mechanisms of misogyny imperils her socially-constructed sex. Why else are feminists so consistently de-sexed in the popular imagination?

Feminism is construed as a threat to femininity when it is, in fact, a threat to gender as labour capital. Women of all ages who fear identifying with feminism cite the popular stereotype of feminists as hairy-legged, loose-breasted, man-hating or man-repelling lesbians who wear that most thuggishly androgyne of sartorial statements, dungarees. The stereotype has persisted for a reason: because it terrorises women with the fear that *radical politics will destroy their sexuality and gender identity*.

Powerful women in the public eye, especially those who lobby for women's rights, are subjected to tirades about their supposedly 'masculine' appearance and behaviour. Women fear abandoning our performative and submissive behaviours because we fear losing our sex. This is a legitimate fear. Women's liberation does indeed constitute a challenge to the capitalist construction of gendered labour, however pleasant it may be to imagine that feminism can be done in five-hundred-dollar Manolos.

The second-wave feminine essential

Second-wave feminism posited a reclamation of the feminine essential as an answer to the submissive, spayed, stilettoed stereotype of misogynist fantasy. An understanding that women's bodies are arrogated spaces of political control made it easy for feminism to fall back on female body essentialism as the solution to patriarchal power. The notion, first posited by second-wave feminists, is that that behind the misogynist packaging of shoes, shopping and bland sexual stereotyping there is a 'real' feminine essential, centred in the 'real' female body, that would heal the hurt of centuries of oppression if we could only access it. This notion is utterly misplaced.

A **fantasy feminine essential**, set against patriarchal feminine constructions and placed in binary opposition to the masculine, was never going to be an adequate foil to the machinations of capitalist patriarchy. The feminine as fact and as ideology is too dispersed and too pervasive for any one 'feminist' physicality to suffice. Too often, bodily essentialism disguises a retreat: a retreat from the politics of capital and labour, a retreat from the broader structures of women's oppression, and a retreat from the true complexities of gender and sexuality. It is not enough, in short, to reclaim the female body as a site of power: we must also ask what the female body is, who has one, and how it is made.

Transsexual dialectics

Germaine Greer wrote in *The Female Eunuch* that "The castration of women has been carried out in terms of a masculine-feminine polarity." The appropriate response to psychological castration, however, is not aggressive maintenance of that polarity – nor can sex alone hold back the rampant, sterilising frigidity of capitalist gender ideals.

The inadequacy of logic in traditional feminist thought about gender and sex is most self-evident when we come, as we must, to the trans question.

The ideological status of trans women has rent stultifying schisms in feminist dialectic. High-profile thinkers such as Mary Daly, Germaine Greer, Janice Raymond, Julie Bindel and even Gloria Steinem have spoken out against what Greer terms "people who think they are women, have women's names, and feminine clothes and lots of eyeshadow, who seem to us to be some kind of ghastly parody."

Some prominent radical feminists have publicly declared that trans women are misogynist, "mutilated men" in awkward dresses attempting to violently penetrate the sacred space of female physical mystery. Greer's orthodoxy that trans women are simply men who seek surgery because they believe that womanhood is akin to male castration has been supplemented with charges that trans people are merely repressed homosexuals who would rather change their physical sex than live in same-sex relationships. Raymond, who was active in campaigns to deny federal funding to sex-change surgery and to force trans women out of influential roles in women's culture, claimed that trans women are "trojan horses of the patriarchy", committing rape by their very existence.[12]

Transsexual people have responded to this harassment by demanding that anti-trans feminists be denied platforms to speak on other issues and, in some cases, by renouncing feminism altogether. The deep personal and ideological wounds inflicted on both sides of the argument are reopened with vigour every time the mainstream press gives space to an anti-trans article by a cis (non-transsexual) feminist.

Many otherwise sensible and learned feminists have fallen prey to lazy transphobic thinking. In the vast majority of cases, feminist transphobia does not stem from deep, personal hatred of trans people, but from drastic, tragic ideological misapprehension of the issues at stake. In 2009, Julie Bindel declared in an article for Standpoint magazine: "The Gender Recognition Act [a UK act which allows people to change sex and be issued with a new birth certificate] will have a profoundly negative effect on the human rights of women and children." Her views are founded on the assumption that "transsexualism, by its nature, promotes the idea that it is 'natural' for boys to play with guns and girls to play with Barbie dolls... the idea that gender roles are biologically determined rather than socially constructed is the antithesis of feminism."[13]

Bindel and others have, initially with the best of intentions, misunderstood not only the nature of transsexualism but also the radical possibilities for gender revolution that real, sisterly alliance between cis feminists and the trans movement could entail.

Binary femininity is a social construct and anti-trans feminists are right to identify it as such: human biology is not subject to cultural norms of gender polarity, and there is a small but significant no-man's land of people who are intersex and hermaphrodite between the male and female sexes. When it comes to re-enforcing damaging stereotypes, however, trans men and women are no guiltier than cis men and women. In fact, the misogyny and sexist stereotyping that Bindel identifies as associated with trans identities are entirely imposed on the trans community by external forces.

Sally Outen, a trans rights campaigner, explains: "It is only natural for a person who strongly wishes to be identified according to her or his felt gender to attempt to provide cues to make the process easy for those who interact with her or him. That person cannot be blamed for the stereotypical nature of the cues that society uses, or if they can be blamed, then every cisgendered person who uses such cues is equally to blame."

Even a casual assessment of the situation indicates that the problem lies not with transsexual people, but with our entire precarious construction of what is 'male' and what 'female', 'masculine' and 'feminine'. Bindel's description of trans women in "fuck-me-boots and birds-nest hair" are no different from today's bewildered 12-, 13- and 14-year-old cissexual girls struggling to make the transition from deeply felt, little-understood womanhood to socially dictated, artificial 'femininity'. Like teenage girls stuffing their bras with loo-roll and smearing on garish lipstick, the trans women for whom Bindel, Greer and their ilk reserve special disdain are simply craving what most growing girls crave: the pathological trappings of gendered social acceptance.

Amy, a 41-year-old trans woman, says: "Transition in later life is a really weird experience, in that you're suddenly and unexpectedly plunged into being teenage, plus you have teenage levels of female hormones coursing through your veins. You haven't grown up through the sidling-toward-teenagerhood that girls get, the socialisation and the immersion in society's expectations and realities. Trans women get to learn those, just a quarter of a century late, in my case. The results tend to be a bit wild." Or, as one cis friend of mine put it: "If I'd had the income that some trans people do when I was a teenager, I'd have owned a cupboard full of fuck-me-boots."

Buying and selling gender

The fact that socially acceptable female identity is something that must be purchased and imposed artificially on the flesh is something that trans women understand better than anyone else. If we locate contemporary patriarchal oppression within the mechanisms of global capitalism, the experience of trans women, who can find themselves pressured to spend large amounts of money in order to 'pass' as female, is a more urgent version of the experience of cis women under patriarchal capitalism. In Western societies, where shopping for clothes and makeup is a key coming-of-age ritual for cis women, all people wishing to express a female identity must grapple with the brutal dictats of the beauty, diet, advertising and fashion industries in order to 'pass' as female.

Whilst radical acceptance of mess and fluids and flesh are part of the ideological core of feminist resistance, the biological feminine essentialism of anti-trans feminists and conservatives alike is misplaced. In truth, not a single person on this planet is born a woman. Becoming a woman, for those who willingly or unwillingly submit to the process, is torturous, magical, bewildering and utterly politicised. In the essay "Mama Cash: Buying and Selling Genders", trans author Charlie Anders explains: "Transgender people... understand more than anyone the high cost of gender, having adopted identities as adult neophytes. People often work harder than they think to maintain the boy/girl behaviours expected of them. You may have learned through painful trial-and-error not to use certain phrases, or to walk a certain way. After a while, learned gender behaviour becomes almost second nature, like trying to compensate for a weak eye. Again, transgender people are just experiencing what everyone goes through."[14]

The concept and practice of sex reassignment surgery (SRS) is the territory over which 'radical' feminists and trans activists traditionally clash most painfully. Bindel, along with others, believes that the fact that SRS is carried out at all means "we've given up on the distress felt by people who identify as gender dysphoric, and turned to surgery instead of trying to find ways to make people feel good in the bodies they have."

Bindel makes the case that the SRS 'industry' is part of a social discourse in which homosexual and gender-non-conforming men and women are brought back into line by "psychiatrists who think that carving people's bodies up can somehow make them 'normal'". Were SRS an accepted way of policing the boundaries of gender non-conformity here, Bindel, Daly, Greer and Raymond's equation of the surgery with 'mutilation' would be more than valid - it would be urgent. However, SRS is nothing of the sort.

In fact, SRS is carried out only very rarely, and only on a small proportion of trans people, for whom the surgery is not a strategy for bringing their body in line with their gender performativity but a way of healing a distressing physical dissonance that Outen vividly describes as "a feeling like I was being raped by my own unwanted anatomy".

Surgery is normally a late stage of the transitioning process and falls within a spectrum of lifestyle choices - for those who opt for it at all. Trans activist Christine Burns points out:

Julie Bindel is quite right that we ought to be able to build a society where people can express the nuances of their gender far more freely, without feeling any compulsion to have to change their bodies more than they really want to.

However, that is precisely what many trans people really do. Only one in five of the people who go to gender clinics have reassignment surgery – the other four in five find accommodations with what they've got. Bindel's thinking cannot admit that, far from emphasising the binary, 80% of trans people are doing far more to disrupt gender stereotypes than she imagines. With or without surgery, trans people are living examples of the fact that gender is variable and fluid.

Of course, like any other surgery, SRS has its risks, and a minority of patients will regret the procedure. But for most of the trans people who decide to pursue SRS, the operation allows for potentially life-saving progression beyond the debilitating effects of gender dysphoria. Moreover, many post-operative trans people have found that the operation actually lessens their overall distress around binary gender identity. Amy explains: "'Being female is an important part of my identity, but it's not an all-consuming part any more. Until I transitioned and completed surgery, it was much more so. I woke up from surgery, and the burning dissonance, the feeling of everything being wrong, wasn't there any more. These days, I realise that I don't actually have that strong a sense of gender any more. Isn't that strange, given all I went through to get here?"

The radical gender fluidity within the trans movement is exactly what Bindel, when I spoke to her in the process of writing this book, emphasised above everything else: "Normality is horrific. Normality is what I, as a political activist, am trying to turn around. Gender bending, people living outside their prescribed gender roles, is fantastic – and I should know. I've never felt like a woman, or like a man for that matter – I don't know what that's supposed to mean. I live outside of my prescribed gender roles, I'm not skinny and presentable, I don't wear makeup, I'm bolshie, I don't behave like a 'real woman', and like anyone who lives outside their prescribed gender roles, I get stick for it."

What Bindel has failed to grasp is that trans people, far from "seeking to become stereotypical", are often as eager to live outside their prescribed gender roles as she is, and just as frustrated by the conformity that a misogynist society demands from those who wish to 'pass'. Marja Erwin told me that "gender identity and gender roles are not the same. I am trans, and I am not the hyperfeminine stereotype. I am a tweener dyke and more butch than femme. I know other trans womyn who are solidly butch, and others who are totally femme, and, of course, the equivalents among straight and bi womyn."

Much of the stereotyping imposed upon trans women is enforced by sexist medical establishments – a phenomenon which radical feminists and trans activists are unanimous in decrying. Bindel, like many trans feminists, objects to the fact that psychiatrists are "allowed to define the issue of gender deviance", giving medical professionals social and ideological influence beyond their professional remit. Clinics in the UK require trans people to fulfil a rigid set of box-ticking gender-performance criteria before they will offer treatment and SRS demands this conformity with special rigour. To receive SRS, trans women patients will normally be expected to have 'lived as a woman' for two years or more – but individual psychiatrists and doctors will get to decide what 'living as a woman' entails. A UK psychiatrist is known to have refused treatment because a trans woman patient turned up to an appointment wearing trousers, whilst Kasper, a trans man who was treated in Norway, was pressured to stop dating men by surgery gatekeepers. "I had to answer a lot of invasive questions about my sexuality and my sex life, and one of the doctors I had to see lectured me about how transitioning physically might make me stop being attracted to boys," he says.

The demand that trans people conform to gender stereotypes in order to be considered 'healthy' or 'a good treatment prospect' is part of an experience that cis women also experience in their dealings with the psychiatric profession. It is standard practice for women in some inpatient treatment facilities to be pressured to wear makeup and dresses as a sign of 'psychological improvement'.

Real female bodies?

Feminists – even prominent ones with big platforms to shout from – do not get to be the gatekeepers of what is and is not female, what is and is not feminine, any more than patriarchal apologists do. Intrinsic to feminism is the notion that such gatekeeping is sexist, recalcitrant and damaging. If feminists like Greer, Bindel and Jan Raymond truly believe that having a vagina, breasts, curves, a uterus, being fertile or sporting several billion XX chromosomes is what makes a person a woman, it clearly sucks to be one of the significant proportion of women who have none of these things.

There are women all over the world who lack breasts following mastectomy or a quirk of biology; women who are born without vaginas, or who are victims of female genital mutilation; women who are androgynously skinny, naturally or because of illness; women who have had hysterectomies; women who are infertile or post-menopausal; or the vast spectrum of women who are biologically intersex, who make up 0.2% of women worldwide. Is the female identity of these people under question too? If it is, feminism has a long way to go.

Greer and her followers seem singularly uninterested in the science behind their binary thinking, which establishes that prescribed gender roles still fall largely into the binary categories of 'man' and 'woman', but human bodies do no such thing. The spectrum of human physicality **belies binary** gender essentialism – as must feminism, if it is ever to be the revolutionary movement our culture so desperately needs.

Trans activism is not merely a valid part of the feminist movement: it is a vital one. The notion that one's biological sex does not have to dictate anything about one's behaviour, appearance or the eventual layout of one's genitals and secondary sex organs, now that we live in a glittering future where such things are possible, is the radical heart of feminist thought.

At the very heart of sexist thought is the notion that the bodies we are born with ought to dictate our character, our behaviour, our appearance, our choices, the nature of our relationships and the work of our lives. Feminism puts forward the still-radical notion that this is not the case. Feminism holds that gender identity, rather than being written in our genes, is an emotional, personal and sexual state of being that can be expressed in myriad different ways that encompass and extend beyond the binary categories of 'man' and 'woman'. Feminism holds that prescribed gender roles are a tyranny that no-one – whether trans, cis, male, female or intersex – should be forced to conform to in order to prove their identity, their validity or their human worth.

Trans feminist revolutions

Feminism calls for gender revolution, and gender revolution needs the trans movement. We must put aside the hurts of the past and look towards a future of radical solidarity between all those who are troubled by gender in the modern world. Whatever our differences, until contemporary feminism fully and finally accepts trans people as ideological allies, it will never achieve what Germaine Greer, Gloria Steinem, Christine Burns, Sally Outen and every feminist who has ever longed for a better world are all working towards: an end to the damaging and demeaning tyranny of gender stereotypes and a coherent resistance to bodily marginalisation.

What part of female experience do trans women not know? How to bleed between the legs? How to adopt a posture of subservience in order to be accepted as one's felt gender? How to ape commercial sexuality and spend money on the trappings of femininity as sanctioned by the overculture? How to perform, and how to long for the freedom to be oneself without having to perform? Trans women know all of these things, many of them better than cis women, because they have had to fight at every turn even for the constrained right to consumer femininity. All women have to fight for gender capital: trans women merely start out in debit.

The one thing that most trans women largely do not experience is reproductive tyranny, the obscenity of living in a culture that tries to stamp itself all over one's womb and clamp itself around one's ovaries and shame XX-genotype women for owning bodies that can create new life. I have stood on too many protest lines beside transsexual women, screaming together for the right to legal abortion on demand after forty years of fighting, to imagine for one second that this is a part of women's oppression that trans women do not understand. The struggle for medical and legal recognition of trans women's needs and the struggle for medical and legal recognition of a woman's right to choose are part of the same dialectic of wresting back state control over women's bodies.

Trans women and transvestites are despised by gender fascists because they do something unforgivable: they take the rules of the game and they make them explicit. They show that femininity is a mode of being that can and must be purchased. They take the sexual sell and they make it manifest, with the courage and ingenuity that often comes from feeling oneself an outsider from the first. And for this reason, almost as a form of patriarchal revenge, violence is enacted upon the bodies of trans women with frequency and force experienced by no other group of women apart from those who work in the sex trade.

Transsexual women and women who sell sex own bodies which

are explicitly – rather than implicitly – part of the brutal capitalist exchange of gender signs. It is seen as somehow apt that these women should apologise for themselves. It is seen as somehow understandable that violence should be done to them on a scale unimaginable even for cis women. Across the world, prostitutes and transsexual women are murdered at horrifying rates. In a recent report for the police district of Columbia, it was estimated that 10-20% of all violent hate crime was targeted at trans women, despite the relatively small size of the trans community in the area.[15] Trans women are murdered so frequently that since 1998, a dedicated day of remembrance has been held every year on November the 20th to draw international attention to the problem of violence against trans people.

Writer and trans activist Julia Serano memorably called attention to trans women as the "whipping girls" of Western culture.[16] The bodies of transsexual women are marginalised and punished precisely because they expose the mechanisms by which the modern carapace of gender capital is maintained, threatening its hold over women's bodies.

4
Dirty Work

The most elementary demand is not the right to work or receive equal pay
for work, but the right to equal work itself
Juliet Mitchell

Marginalised bodies do marginalised work. Bodies that are arrogated and controlled can be persuaded to do work that is underpaid and overlooked. Slavemaking is a social science, and nowhere is that science more expertly demonstrated than in the continued ability of contemporary industrial culture to persuade women perform the vast majority of vital domestic and caring labour without expecting reward or payment.

After a century of feminism, women still do the lion's share of caring, cooking and cleaning duties, for free. Nowadays, we are also encouraged to do 'real' work – i.e., work traditionally done by men, outside the home – on top of these domestic duties, albeit for less pay and fewer rewards. In 2003, British women still performed an average of nineteen hours' worth of housework per week, compared with only five hours for men, whose share of the domestic burden has remained essentially unchanged since the early 1980s.[17] Whilst unemployment and retirement decreased the number of hours spent by men on domestic work, they increased women's hours.

Women's work-relationship to their bodies mirrors our work-relationship to our homes: we labour at great personal cost to gild our cages, our increasing resentment tempered by fear of the social consequences of refusal. This fear is engendered in us by patriarchal capitalism, which would have everything to lose were women to once refuse to perform for free all the boring domestic work vital to support alienated industrial labour. We tidy away the messy reality of our bodies just as we tidy away the grim reality of domestic toil, because have been schooled to fear losing our womanhood, losing our identity, if we refuse to shape up and clean house, no matter what our other engagements of paid work and social interaction may be. Modern women are told that we can have it all, which in practice means that *we must and should do it all – with a smile, and for free.*

There was once a dedicated movement, tied in to Marxist feminism, to change the labour conditions of working women across the world. This movement petered out in the 1980s, despite the fact that the labour dispute on the domestic front was never close to being won. Instead, men and women have retreated into a grim stalemate, and many find themselves standing on a picket line that extends across every home, from the sink to the washing machine to the kids' bedrooms. Before we set up homes together, we may not be aware that this picket line exists, but the strategic socio-sexual marginalisation of women's bodies makes it seem somehow natural and right that all the dirty, messy work of the home should be performed by women for low pay or no pay. Women are seen as animalistic, manipulable, and born to be low-paid workers; because we see ourselves in that way too, we capitulate - we abandon our resistance in effect, we scab.

Domestic drudgery is a capitalist construction

Whilst researching this chapter I interviewed Western women of all ages and classes who were balancing domestic labour with paid, 'real' work, and my overwhelming impression was one of defeatism and paralysis. Women, whether or not they identify as feminists, feel guilt about the state of our homes in the same way that we feel guilt about the state of our bodies – we feel ashamed of being seen to have somehow lost control, to be insufficiently worthy of our womanhood as socially interpreted. "Not being able to keep one's house clean still suggests complete breakdown," says Lucy, 38, a full-time mother. "Every time a stranger comes to my door I worry that they are glancing past me at the grubby porch, and sofa covered in dog-fur and thinking, 'that woman has lost control of her life.' I feel like if my elderly neighbour looks in, she'll think I'm a failure as a woman." The feminization of domestic labour makes makes it seem at once trivial and an essential part of female identity. Housework and childcare are not real work, because women do them – and because they are done by women, whose bodies are marginalised to the point of unreality, they are not real work.

In fact, domestic labour is not at all trivial. Without the work that women do for free, every western economy would collapse within days. In the United States, the money that women should in theory be owed for their unpaid caring and domestic work runs to some six times the national defence budget, and the US defence budget is not small.

There is a word for what happens when you trap someone within the confines of a house and make them work for no reward for generations and tell them that they're good for nothing else. There's a word for what happens when generations of children of both sexes are raised in environments underpinned by resentment and the control dynamics essential to getting women's work done for nothing. There's a word for what happens when home and work in the home becomes indelibly associated with self-negation, abuse and stifled rage, and the word is trauma. The entirety of Western society is still traumatised by our complex relationship to the economics of domestic labour. No family truly escapes.

To understand why we are so dreadfully messed up when it comes to the entire sphere of life involving necessary care and self-care, it's vital to comprehend that we are living in a culture that has been traumatised – emotionally, physically, sexually and psychologically traumatised. At the 2009 Compass Conference women's seminar, speakers from the floor asked why housework is still so undervalued. It is undervalued because we have, slowly but surely, turned home itself into a locus of slavery, suffering and trauma. No wonder men are scared of scrubbing floors. Feminism did not do this.

The c-word: rewriting history.

Capitalism is the essential context for understanding the marginalisation of women's bodies within the home. It was, after all, industrial capitalism which created and perpetuated the conditions for the degradation of housework and the degradation of women by association.

Historians such as Leonore Davidoff and Catherine Hall have described how separate spheres for men and women emerged between 1780 and 1850 as the workplace became separated from the home and a private, domestic sphere was created for women, formally and symbolically severing the processes of production and reproduction.[18] The simple work of creating and sustaining life does not fit within the profit-oriented, pay-and-target driven capitalist imagining of society, but that work still had to be done, and it had to be done away from the factory floor, which after child labour laws came into force over the first half of the 19th century was officially declared no place for children. Thus, in 1737 over 98 per cent of married women in England worked outside the home, but by 1911 over 90 per cent were employed solely as housewives. Ivan Illich calls this process "the enclosure of women".[19]

The divorce of the domestic front from the public world of profit-oriented work and citizenship was reaffirmed by important new legal sanctions: married women were officially forbidden from owning property or making contracts, shutting them out from the world of business, and the 1832 Reform Bill made women's exclusion from political citizenship explicit for the first time, formally isolating women within the confines of the home.

In her editorial to *New Internationalist*'s issue on the politics of housework, Debbie Taylor explains that "though domestic work has existed ever since there was a domus in which to do it, the housewife role is a very recent one indeed – and confined to industrialized societies."[20] As sociologist Anne Oakley put it, "other cultures may live in families but they do not necessarily have housewives. They have women, men and children whose labour is woven together like coloured thread in a tapestry, creating home, life and livelihood for the whole family."[21] As it became necessary for domestic work to be shoehorned cheaply into the profit-margins of industrial society, history was rapidly rewritten to ensure the acceptance of housework as woman's divinely decreed role.

Just as this brutal domestic binary was made concrete, Darwin careered into the ideological landscape, crushing amongst other things the old Judeo-Christian excuses for female domesticity. A new logical basis for housework was needed, and fast. So the 'hunter-gatherer' mythos of human prehistoric development as extricated from the Christian imagining of history began to be phrased explicitly as dichotomy: male hunters versus female gatherers. Even the importance to some academic schools of the idea of human society as matriarchal and goddess-worshipping in the Paleolithic era has not diminished the notion that early female 'gathering' involved childcare, cooking, sewing and cleaning and, in the case of Wilma Flintstone, wearing stone-cut stilettos and brandishing a mini-mammoth vacuum cleaner: occupations that actually endorse not prehistoric but post-industrial norms of 'feminine' behaviour. The separation of the world of work into the superior productive and inferior reproductive, domestic sphere is not inherent to human organisation: it is a new thing. Over the course of centuries, the mechanisms of industrial capitalism and associated urbanisation have narrowed the concept of home to the confines of a house, creating in the process a system of battery pens for forced female labour. No wonder nobody wants to do the dishes any more.

Following the revolutionary feminism of the 1960s that began in the domestic prisons of the white middle-classes, the sheen has long since faded from the gilded cage of domesticity. Both men and women can now clearly see the trap into which 'domestic' labour has been fashioned. But our response to this as decent, thinking beings has been woefully lacking. Feminism has achieved a vital expansion in women's labour outside the home – but it has not won the corresponding, equally vital expansion of men's labour within it. Feminism has amended the old patriarchal deal, but it has not ended it.

Mutually assured dysfunction

One of the most difficult things for feminists to acknowledge is the real harm done by women as well as by men in the domestic sphere. Partly as a consequence of hard-packed resentment at cultural isolation and forced drudgery, generations of women – mothers in particular – have handed down suffering, guilt and the expectation of patriarchal servitude to their children with a breathtaking ruthlessness borne of love and shame. Amanpreet Badyal, 21, told me how her childhood was blighted by her mother's anguish:

My mother has tried repeatedly to break my spirit, claiming that she's just preparing me for my mother-in-law. Alongside this, she harangued both my sisters to learn to cook; despite both successfully doing so, she subsequently tried to blame all marital problems, especially my eldest sister's, on cooking. The thing is, my mum means well. She had seen what it is like for us Punjabi women, the sham of Sikh equality, and she wanted there to be no hope to so cruelly give way, treacherously feather-light, to betrayal and disappointment. I sincerely believed that I would never make it to 21, and that if I did, I would find myself in a marriage that would eventually drive me to suicide. How could I continue my mother's cycle, and raise children that I resented? Why would I want to raise another child like myself, plagued by self-doubt and devoured by the family pack? I was hellishly afraid of this happening to me.

A blunt instrument for undermining gender activism and feminist solidarity is the claim that such assaults on human dignity are 'cultural', and therefore sacrosanct. In fact, not only is culture not a trump card in the progressive ideological battle, the isolation of women in the home and the traumatising of the domestic sphere are not unique to Sikh culture, or to 'Asian' culture, or to any culture not immediately comprehensible to middle-class white people. On the contrary, they are common throughout Western society, and have been a central narrative fact of the last 350 years of Western history.

Only saints react to imprisonment and abuse without retaliation, and women are not saints. The stereotype of the angel in the home was always a lie: for generations, and particularly since the post-war enforced domesticity of the 1950s, women have reacted to their domestic cages with a rage and resentment that has been at once effortlessly political and unguessably damaging. Given power in the domestic sphere and only there, limited, anxious matriarchies have developed across Western societies, and everyone understands what it means to have an Italian Mother, a Greek Mother, a Jewish Mother, or any other racist variation on the harridan hypothesis. The truth, however, is that the fury of female emotional control in the post-industrial home is the fury of the worker alienated from the means of production and reproduction, a fury deliberately weighted against the cruelty of male political and economic dominance in public society. Thus it is that 21st-century capitalism maintains a structure of gendered labour in which everyone, male or female, is to some extent powerless and to some extent miserable.

It is this dichotomy of dysfunction which is truly challenged by gay and single-parent families. When conservative pundits tell us that lone and homosexual parents represent a threat to 'family values', they are articulating this basic fear – that the structures of mutual repression will be broken by people brave enough to create and live in homes which challenge the culture and economics of that system.

I am the child and grandchild of housewives who hated housework. My grandmother, who as I write this chapter is in the latter stages of terminal cancer, did her duty as an immigrant Catholic homemaker, raising six children in a tiny council house in Bristol. A bright and beautiful woman who loved learning, Marta Penny ought to have gone to university, but her infant ambition was quickly crushed by the commandment to wield socio-economic power only and forever in the fantasy Catholic home. The frustrations of received femininity have defined my grandmother: her entire life has been undercut by misery, resentment and passive-aggression, instilled into her from her childhood in Malta, where her own mother made her scrub the floors daily with an old toothbrush to get her 'used' to drudgery.

Her youngest daughter, my mother, is a brilliant defence lawyer who put her career on hold to take care of my sisters and myself, having given up on getting my father to do his share. Raised with the belief that women deserved to be educated and to earn money, she was shocked to find herself facing the same frustrations that plagued her mother, frustrations which were lessened only after her divorce.

Beyond the gilded cage

In one way or another, the domestic deal makes cowards of us all. Betty Friedan's *The Feminine Mystique* lit the fuse which blew the cage door open in the 1960s and 1970s, but we have failed, like tame animals, to step very far across the threshold of that cage. Our labour battles are tentative, and we are slow to apprehend our own bargaining power.

I asked hundreds of women, married and single, living with their partners and living with housemates, in Europe and North America and Australia, about how they organised their domestic labour and whether their partners shared the load. Hundreds of times over, the answer was almost identical: "He just can't cope with the dishes";

"He doesn't understand how to sort laundry no matter how many times I explain it"; "He says he can't do it, which is his way of saying that he won't do it". Most of all: "He says he can't see the dirt I see". One woman cried as she told me how she and her disabled mother had no choice but to cook, clean and care for a recalcitrant alcoholic father and two brothers, on top of being a single mother and student herself. "It actually is a war," she said.

Anyone who has ever been seven years old knows when "can't" really means "won't". What at first seemed to be individual grudges amongst the women and girls I interviewed turned out to be a universal complaint: even though they know perfectly well that there is no logical reason for them to be exempt from the sponge and the loo brush, all that men and boys have to do to avoid chores is dig in their heels and refuse to acknowledge the dirt; sit and moulder in their own accumulating grime; wait out the filth. Eventually, a nearby female will reluctantly roll up her dainty sleeves and wipe up the mess.

It is not so much that men have a higher tolerance for dirt – on the contrary, recent studies have shown that roughly the same percentage of adult men and women care "a lot or quite a lot" about standards of hygiene and domestic comfort. Rather, domestic equality stumbles against the fact that men, as members of the domestic bourgeois, have so much more to lose as individuals and as a privileged group by facing up to the base cowardice of that 'can't'. What we are facing here is not series of separate household slanging matches but a systemic offensive against women's rights as workers.

My generation, born after the supposed victory of feminism, grew up with that labour dispute on our doorsteps, our infant identities held hostage in the subtle violence of domestic negotiations. Kathryn, 35, from Winnipeg, Canada, is just one of the growing army of women who will do anything not to have to bear the pain and frustration that our mothers faced:

My mother seemed to be tired and stressed out pretty much all the time. I don't remember her being happy often. I honestly think that by the end of the day, she had nothing left to give us, emotionally speaking – she was worn out, and even the fact that she was out there earning a paycheque had no appreciable impact on her total responsibility on the domestic front. Watching my mother become a tired automaton had a huge impact on my life. I vowed never to end up with a man who didn't do his share. I failed at that the first time, and I ended up hiring a cleaner to save my marriage. I couldn't stand that he wilfully ignored dirt, and I couldn't stand things only got done if I had a meltdown. I feel very strongly that my girls should see me smile and laugh as often as possible. I give them a lot of physical affection and tell them I love them every day, because I don't want them to feel the lack I did.

Big babies

There are, of course, some occasions when 'can't' really does mean 'can't'. And this should give us pause for thought. Why, in a culture which has had universal electrical provision for barely seventy years, do so many men lack the basic practical skills to prevent themselves and their loved ones starving, freezing, sickening, burning or choking to death in their own homes?

Like any bourgeois class, men have been kept ignorant and dependent on a class of labourers with subordinated bodies, and encouraged to see that ignorance and that dependence as empowerment. Boys in the post-war era in particular have been denied even the basic tools of housekeeping, and three generations of young men have now grown up watching their fathers do next to nothing in the home, apart from the sanctioned male activities of lawn maintenance and garden barbecue operation. Keeping men dependent on women to take care of them reinforces the double-headed axe of domestic disenfranchisement, ensuring that post-industrial capitalist homemaking is seen as the only viable option for people who want to live comfortable lives and raise healthy families.

The genius of this strategy has been to persuade men that their learned incompetence in the home is strength, when in fact it is weakness – terrible weakness. That weakness places immeasurable restrictions on the choices of men and boys both within and outside the home.

The deliberate domestic disempowerment of men did not begin with no-fault divorce laws. On the contrary – the empowerment which men really have lost in the home is not about dominance, but about self-sufficiency: not a man's right to sit at the head of the table or to have 'access' to 'his' children, but the power to cook a meal that feeds a family or to keep himself and his loved ones from squalor and sickness. For many years, men and boys have been deliberately deprived of these skills, and adult men and women have colluded in that deprivation, which is two-horned in its faulty logic: not only are domestic work, childcare and homemaking beneath the dignity of men, but men themselves are apparently congenitally incapable of performing these tasks. How many times have you heard a home-based woman say, her resentment tinged with a hint of pride, that her husband just can't take care of himself – or, if he sometimes deigns to do the dishes, that he's 'well trained'? How many times have you heard a man refer to taking care of his own children as 'babysitting'?

Just as the lie of male domestic disempowerment flatters men that they are more suited to directly profit-producing work, it flatters women that housework is somehow their special inheritance, that their men are in some way genetically inferior, categorically incapable of taking proper care of themselves or anyone else.

Meanwhile, the most brain-bleedingly pointless domestic tasks have, for some young women today, become so alien and fantastic that they are now a lifestyle option. Cookery classes and knitting circles encourage young, trendy western women to indulge in a sanctioned fantasy of glamorous domesticity that never really existed, an arched, kinky fetishism of the trappings of a drudgery that is still the reality of many women's lives. I know plenty of young women my age, educated and emancipated, who view the baking of immaculate muffins and the embroidering of intricate scarves and mittens as exciting hobbies, pastimes which should be properly performed in high-waisted fifties skirts and silly little pinafores. Oddly enough, most of these women have no more of a clue how to iron the pleats into a pair of dress trousers than I do. Such hedonistic time-wastage has all the historical accuracy of the sort of sexual role-play which involves Victorian schoolboy outfits and birch whipping canes, and like all such power-play, the practice is perfectly jolly fun as long as it isn't taken seriously. Unexamined, there is always the risk that a fetish will bleed into reality.

Working 9 to 5

In industrial capitalist society, waged work is the only strategy for being acknowledged and acknowledging yourself as fully human. As such, the struggles of women for equal pay and equal opportunities in the job market and the struggles of women to be recognised as human beings in their own right have been seen by many both within and outside the feminist movement as one and the same. In fact, they are nothing of the kind. Women are people whether we are waged or unwaged, working full time as business leaders or as mothers, whether we support ourselves financially, are supported by family members, or receive state benefits; all women are people, just as all people are people. Similarly, the right to equal pay for equal work, still a hurdle Western women have yet to surmount, is a struggle that is important on its own merits, because it is about basic fairness, not because waged work is what validates our very existence. We deserve equal pay because it is our right as workers: we do not require it to justify our humanity.

At some point during the 1990s, the international Wages For Housework campaign, once a key part of the feminist agenda, dragged itself into a corner and quietly died. The campaign, stolidly opposed even by right-thinking hand-wringing liberals in its day, is now universally acknowledged as preposterously unrealistic – not because it isn't women's moral right to receive rewards for their labour above and beyond the satisfaction of a job well done, but because no modern government can afford to pay its women for the lifetimes of work they do for free.

Passing the buck

Sadly, the trench warfare that currently has men terrified into refusing housework and women longing to rid themselves of it is pernicious enough that very many women would rather be complicit in the exploitation of other, poorer women than confront their own partners. The questions that Jane Story posed when writing for New Internationalist in 1988 are still hanging: "It appears that women professionals – feminist and non-feminist alike – have solved their personal housework crisis in the easiest way possible. They've simply bought their way out of the problem. Instead of being exploited themselves, they shift the exploitation to another woman. But not everyone can pass the buck in this way. Who cleans the cleaner's house?"[22]

Of the women I spoke to who had found a workable solution to the sharing of domestic work in their households, 90% employed some sort of home help, from a weekly cleaner to a live-in au pair. Many more expressed a hope that they would one day be able to afford similar domestic help. Rich households have always had servants, but the anxiety and reach of contemporary Western women's employment of cleaners and carers to relieve them of the double shift of housework and paid work is unprecedented. This strategy is not without its drawbacks. Hardly any of the women questioned were entirely comfortable with the situation, as well they might not be: nearly all cleaners, childminders and nannies are female, and a large proportion are foreign-born, either legal or illegal migrants. Western women's despair at the very point of asking our male relatives to do their bit, our unwillingness to challenge the system at its root, is such that an entire generation has been willing to simply hand down their oppression to poor, migrant and ethnic minority women.

Whilst most domestics are paid, albeit poorly, a proportion are illegal immigrants controlled by gangs, and some are victims of human trafficking. Although due to the nature of international operations accurate estimates are still impossible, it is believed that fully twelve percent of the 27 million victims of human trafficking worldwide – 700,000 in the United States alone – are indentured domestic slaves. A further 36% are delicately described as 'miscellaneous' or 'other' workers, meaning in plain English that some sex slaves are also expected to wash the sheets afterwards.

It would be soothing to think that the wealthy men and women employing these unfortunate women are largely ignorant of their plight, but this is not the case. In Westernised areas of the Middle East such as Dubai, the burning of domestics' passports is routine – and illegal residence in the country is punishable by death. In 2007, a wealthy couple from Muttontown, New York, were convicted of enslaving and torturing two Indonesian women who were brought to their mansion to work as housekeepers, and similar cases have come to light across the United States since federal anti-trafficking laws were brought into force in the year 2000. Across the world, disgusting damage is inflicted by our unwillingness to confront our terror of gender-specified drudgery.

Judith Ramirez, co-ordinator of the Toronto-based International Coalition to End Domestics' Exploitation (INTERCEDE) insists that there is no simple solution to what she calls "a modern day variation on the slave trade" – hiring a nanny or a housekeeper is really a question of women trying to fend for themselves. "I don't see any other way when there are so few day-care places for young children. We're nowhere near a universal day-care system accessible to everyone. As long as that's the case, there are going to be a lot of women hired as domestics."

Men and women have been passing the buck for too long. We need to confront our own hypocrisy and find equable, less exploitative solutions to the dichotomy of domestic dysfunction, before more harm is done.

Marginalised bodies, marginalised work

Every nation relies for its very survival on its female citizens failing, day after day, year after year, generation after generation, to refuse to drudge for no reward. This should, in theory, give women great power, simply by the threat of refusing, one day, to serve.

Female power of refusal is the single most scary, most horrifying, most insistently phobic thing facing any society, ever. Women could, in theory, refuse to cook and clean and care and keep society running. Women could refuse to fit themselves out in conformity with the patriarchal proclivity not just for staid, acceptable sex, but for social order. Women could refuse that vital work, the bearing of children and the raising of future generations, all of which are keyed in to the domestic gender war. Simply by doing nothing at all, women could bring every Western society to its knees tomorrow. That single fact is intolerably terrifying: women must be stopped at all costs from having that basic human right, the right to say no, the right to lay down our tools and pull on our skirts and say, stop. No more. I will not serve.

The very easiest way to deny someone the basic human right of refusal is to deny their personhood and potential. And the easiest way to deny someone their personhood and potential, in contemporary society as in any ancient slaveowning culture, is not to pay them.

We could refuse to serve, of course. But anyone who has internalised even a solitary crumb of the post-industrial gender fetish knows that a woman's power of refusal is circumscribed on every level. In the flesh trade of modern production, women's labour hours, like our bodies, are common property. We all know that when a woman says no, she really means yes.

Conclusion

The neoliberal repugnance for women's bodies must be understood as a fundamental part of the strategies of work and capital that sustain global production. Individual women's anxiety about keeping our own bodies under control is part of the same structure of oppression under whose auspices cultural, physical and sexual violence is done to the bodies of low-status women, poor women, migrant workers, transsexual women, sex workers and every other person living and working at the coalface of the so-called gender war.

The recent revival in feminist sentiment across the West has so far failed to produce an adequate sense of political totality whereby a program for resistance to oppression might be developed. Such resistance is possible, but it will involve a sustained and serious attack on the social basis for control of women's bodies: on work, on domestic labour, on political power and intimacy. This is not a small task, nor one that can be accomplished purely on the basis of individual sexual and physical empowerment.

We cannot fuck our way to freedom. Sexuality alone, and heterosexuality in particular, is never enough to destabilise complex architectures of money and power. Without political agitation, sex can always be co-opted, calcifying gender revolution into another weary parade of saleable binary stereotypes.

We cannot shop our way to freedom. Even if we eventually manage to buy enough shoes, enough makeup and enough confidence-boosting surgical butchery to justify our place in the labour exchange of female beauty, we will find ourselves marginalised by the very process of physical transformation that promised to liberate us.

And we cannot fight the system on our own. Learning not to despise our own flesh is a political statement, and learning to eat and love and nurture ourselves a vital process for any woman wishing to engage positively with the world of power – but however hard we try to love our bodies, it won't make us free. The personal is political, but as far as feminism is concerned, the political need not always collapse into the personal.

Popular culture's insistence on feminine erotic capital is a strategic part of the subsumption of women's labour, and the solution is collective as well as individual. For women, the personal is political precisely because our bodies are a collective site of material production; it follows that if we want to re-enfranchise ourselves, we must collectively refuse to submit to capitalist body orthodoxy. There is nothing more terrifying to a society built on female purchasing power and unpaid labour than the notion that women might refuse to join the sell. Patriarchal capitalism can put up with a great deal of women's chatter as long as we refrain from saying the one word nobody wants to hear from women: the word 'no'.

Contemporary pseudo-feminism is all about the power of yes. Yes, we want shoes, orgasms and menial office work. Yes, we want chocolate, snuggles and straight hair. Yes, we will do all the dirty little jobs nobody else wants to do, yes, we will mop and sweep and photocopy and do the shopping and plan the meals and organise the parties and wipe up all the shit and the dirt and grin and strip and perform and straighten our backs and smile and say yes, again yes, we will do it all. Yes, we will buy, more than anything we will buy what you tell us we need to buy to be acceptable. Yes, the word of submission, the word of coercion and capitulation. Yes, we will fuck you in gorgeous lingerie and yes, we will make you dinner afterwards. Yes, yes, yes, yes, yes!

Body orthodoxy is the base code for this language of coercion, fooling women into the belief that by aligning ourselves within the narrow coffin of acceptable female physicality, by taming our bodies, purchasing the commoditised signs of western femininity and performing our sexuality in the most frigid and alienated of ways, we can lead happy, fulfilling lives. This is manifestly a lie. We can tell that this is a lie, because most women in the West are still tired, unfulfilled and unhappy. However much we shop, screw, starve, sweat and apply make-up to conceal the marks of weariness and unhappiness, however perfectly we submit, the astronomically vast majority of women will never win within the rules of the system as it stands. The capitalist vision of female physical perfection is a shallow grave of frigid signs and brutal rules, signifying only sterility and death. If we want to live, we need to remember the language of resistance.

Only by remembering how to say 'no' will the women of the 21st century regain their voice and remember their power. 'No' is the most powerful word in a woman's dialectic arsenal, and it is the one word that our employers, our leaders and, quite often, the men in our lives would do anything to prevent us from saying. No, we will not serve. No, we will not settle for the dirty work, the low-paid work, the unpaid work. No, we will not stay late at the office, look after the kids, sort out the shopping. We refuse to fit the enormity of our passion, our creativity, and our potential into the rigid physical prison laid down for us since we were small children. No. We refuse. We will not buy your clothes and shoes and surgical solutions. No, we will not be beautiful; we will not be good. Most of all, we refuse to be beautiful and good.

If we want to be free, the women of the 21st century need to stop playing the game. We need to end our weary efforts to believe that our bodies are acceptable and begin to know, with a clear and brilliant certainty, that our persons are powerful.

References

1. Gogoi, P., "I Am Woman, Hear Me Shop", Bloomberg Business Week, February 2005
2. Letts, Q., "The First Ladette: How Germaine Greer's legacy is an entire generation of loose-knickered lady louts," The Daily Mail, 20th November 2009
3. Baudrillard, J., *The Consumer Society: Myths and Structures*, Sage Publications Ltd, 1998
4. Power, N., *One Dimensional Woman*, Zer0 Books, 2009
5. Wolf, N., *The Beauty Myth: How Images Of Beauty Are Used Against Women*, Vintage, 1991
6. Elliott, C. and Schaffauser, T., "Sex Workers Are Not Criminals", The Guardian, 8 March 2010
7. http://www.disordered-eating.co.uk/eating-disorders-statistics/anorexia-nervosa-statistics-us.html
8. Andersen, AE. "Gender-related aspects of eating disorders: a guide to practice," The Journal of Gender-Specific Medicine 1999; 2(1):47-54,
9. Roberts, R., Sanders, T., Smith, D. and Myers, E. *Participation in Sex Work: Students' Views. Sex Education: Sexuality, Society and Learning*, 10(2), 145-156, 2010
10. Tucker, T., *The Great Starvation Experiment: The Heroic Men Who Starved so That Millions Could Live*, Free Press, A Division of Simon & Schuster, Inc., 2006
11. Ryan, T., "Roots of Masculinity" in Metcalf, A. and Humphries, M. (eds.), *The Sexuality of Men*, Pluto, 1985
12. Raymond, J., *The Transsexual Empire: The Making of the She-Male*, Teachers' College Press, 1979
13. Bindel, J., "The Operation That Can Ruin Your Life", Standpoint, November 2009
14. Anders, C., "Mama Cash: Buying and Selling Genders" in

Schalit, J. (ed). *The Anti-Capitalism Reader: Imagining a Geography of Opposition*, Akashic, 2002

15. http://glbt.dc.gov/DC/GLBT/About+GLBT/Publications/ Biased+Crime+Report+Updated+Feb+2010

16. Serano, J., *Whipping Girl: A Transsexual Woman on Sexism and the Scapegoating of Femininity*, Seal Pres, 2007

17. Ramos, X., *Domestic Work Time and Gender Differentials in Great Britain 1992-1998: Facts, value judgements and subjective fairness perceptions*, Essex University, 2003

18, 19. Davidoff, L., *Worlds Between: Historical Perspectives on Gender and Class*, Polity Press, 1995

20, 21, 22. Taylor, D. (ed), *Life Sentence: The Politics of Housework*, New Internationalist Issue 181, March

Contemporary culture has eliminated both the concept of the public and the figure of the intellectual. Former public spaces – both physical and cultural – are now either derelict or colonized by advertising. A cretinous anti-intellectualism presides, cheerled by expensively educated hacks in the pay of multinational corporations who reassure their bored readers that there is no need to rouse themselves from their interpassive stupor. The informal censorship internalized and propagated by the cultural workers of late capitalism generates a banal conformity that the propaganda chiefs of Stalinism could only ever have dreamt of imposing. Zer0 Books knows that another kind of discourse – intellectual without being academic, popular without being populist – is not only possible: it is already flourishing, in the regions beyond the striplit malls of so-called mass media and the neurotically bureaucratic halls of the academy. Zer0 is committed to the idea of publishing as a making public of the intellectual. It is convinced that in the unthinking, blandly consensual culture in which we live, critical and engaged theoretical reflection is more important than ever before.